AIRBRUSH TECHNIQUES

for Waterfowl Carving

Michael Veasey

P9-CCH-438

Preface by William Veasey

Text written with and photography
by Douglas Congdon-Martin

Schiffer Publishing Ltd

1469 Morstein Road, West Chester, Pennsylvania 19380

Copyright © 1992 by Michael Veasey
Library of Congress Catalog Number: 92-60643.

All rights reserved. No part of this work may be reproduced or used in any forms or by any means—graphic, electronic or mechanical, including photocopying or information storage and retrieval systems—without written permission from the copyright holder.

Printed in the United States of America.
ISBN: 0-88740-384-0

We are interested in hearing from authors with book ideas on related topics.

Published by Schiffer Publishing, Ltd.
1469 Morstein Road
West Chester, Pennsylvania 19380
Please write for a free catalog.
This book may be purchased from the publisher.
Please include $2.00 postage.
Try your bookstore first.

Contents

Preface

There has been an increasing need for a book outlining and demonstrating the basic tools and techniques involved in the airbrushing of bird carvings.

Since 1987 Veasey Studios, under the supervision of Michael Veasey, has sealed, undercoated, and accomplished the basic color blending on approximately 40,000 individual carvings, from very simple to complex. With this vast experience it follows logically that Michael be the one to do this book.

We have found that the airbrush is a superior tool for certain tasks. By no means is it meant to replace the brush. Rather it is to be used in combination with the brush to accomplish the smoothest most professional and artistic finished birds.

It is my sincere belief that, if you use the techniques outlined here, your finished carving will be greatly enhanced. Further, it pleases me that a third member of my family now has chosen to add to the literature of the carving field.

William Veasey
Elkton, Maryland

Introduction

While not new, airbrushing is gaining popularity among carvers of decoys and waterfowl. Not only is it faster than brush painting, in many applications it also has tends to bring more realism to the work.

As with any new and unfamiliar thing, there is a natural reluctance to try airbrushing. Part of the problem is the investment of money it requires. A good compressor can cost $200-300, and fancy airbrushes can run over $200. Fortunately, much more moderately priced brushes are all you really need.

Another reason carvers are reluctant is that they don't know how to use the darn thing! On the pages that follow you will see just how easy it really is. With step-by-step instructions, we will take you from the beginning to finishing a drake and hen teal duck. When you are finished I think you will find that the airbrush, when used in conjunction with traditional brush techniques, will add to your joy of carving and the quality of your work.

Paint and Air: The hardest part of airbrushing is getting the paint to the right consistency. Unfortunately, the only way to learn the right way is by trial and error. All the literature tells you to use free flowing paint (the consistency of water), with the air compressor set at 30 lbs of pressure. This is good for tee shirts, but it doesn't work too well on decoys.

For decoys, I find that the paint needs to have the consistency of housepaint. With this mixture and the air pressure at 60-65 lbs the coverage is great, and a lot of problems are eliminated.

I use acrylic paint, which I buy as premixed tube paint and blend to proper color and consistency. Remember it is always easier to thin the paint than to make it thicker. When starting out it is a good idea to make it thicker than you think is necessary, and dilute as you go.

Equipment: I do almost all my work with a Paasche H series airbrush with a number 5 needle. The smaller tips, numbers one and three will clog up too easily, and the number 5 tip can be dialed down to do the fine work you need. The reason I use this model airbrush is the simplicity of taking it apart and cleaning it.

The air compressor should be able to provide at least 60 lbs of pressure. I recommend that the compressor you purchase be ½ horsepower or more, with at least a 10 gallon holding tank.

Airbrushing Basics

The tip consists of the needle,

the color cap,

and the air cap.

The second control on the airbrush is the color cap. By turning it you control the amount of paint flowing through the brush.

This is a double action gun. The air is controlled from this button. The further you depress it, the stronger the flow of air. The small wheel in front of the button is a governor which can be adjusted to limit the flow of air.

This in-line moisture trap helps reduce the amount of moisture from your air source. Because a very small drop of water will ruin fine work, this is an important part of the equipment and should be maintained in working order.

When I am using small amounts of a color, I use a color cup to hold my paints. It is included in every kit.

For the jar to operate efficiently, the little air vent at the top must be open. When it becomes clogged, I simply use a spare piece of eye wire and ream it out.

For decoy and waterfowl work I generally prefer to use three ounce bottles, with one color in each bottle. These are the colors for the green winged teal, and each jar is labeled for convenience.

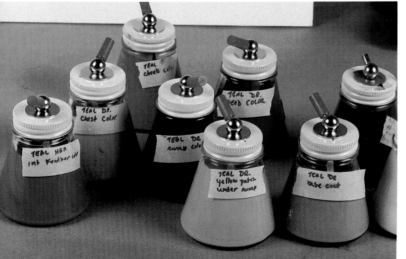

9

With the color cup or jar removed, simply squirt a bit into the back of the tip, and blow some air through the brush. Repeat this procedure until all the color is removed.

To clean the brush between colors, we've found that the product 409™ works the best.

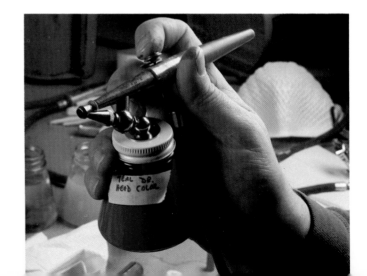

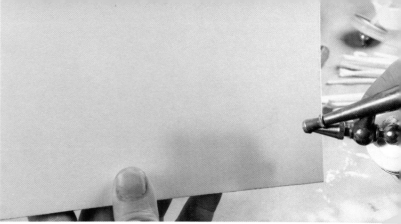

One of the rules of airbrushing waterfowl is to always blend the dark color into the light. Begin by laying down the lighter color. If I want my blend line to be here, about three inches from the edge of the practice board...

I carry my color about an inch or an inch-and one half above this line, into the area that will be painted the darker shade.

Opposite page, bottom right:
Hold the air brush with your ring and little fingers around the body pressing it against your palm, your middle finger tucked under the brush, your forefinger on the button, and your thumb supporting the brush.

I then fill in all with the lighter color.

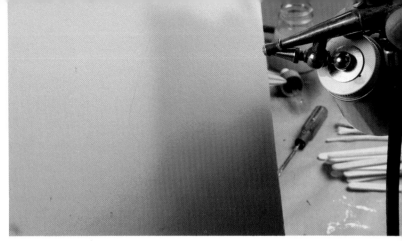

At first the area is likely to look blotchy.

Continue to fill in until the color is consistent and smooth.

Before changing colors, put your finger over the end of the brush and push the air button.

This cleans paint out of the knuckle at the top of the jar so it does not clog.

To thin the paint, simply add a few drops of water. Be careful not to add too much at one time. It is much easier to thin the paint than it is to make it thicker.

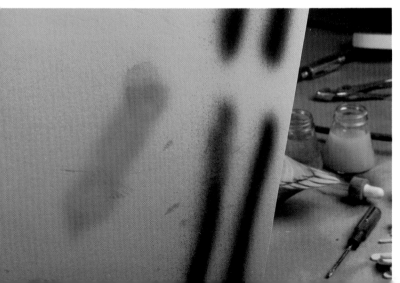

Always test your paint before using it on your carving. When I switched to the darker color I got this splattered effect. This means that the paint is too thick.

Start the darker color at the blend line and move into the dark area. To get the blended effect you want, hold the airbrush about five inches from the work at the blend line.

Fill in as you go. You see we have a dark line developing.

To fix this, hold the airbrush further away from the work and mist the color onto the surface.

As you work closer to the blend line, hold the airbrush further from the work.

To make dots, hold the airbrush about ½ to ¾ inch away from the surface, and shoot short bursts of paint.

The blended surface of the practice board.

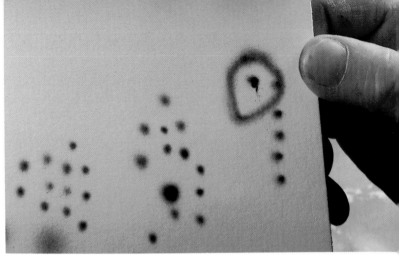

If the paint is too wet, it is likely to run like this.

The further you are from the surface, the larger the dot will be.

If it is too thick it will splatter like this. You will need to practice to get both the technique and the paint consistent to work properly.

Airbrushing Waterfowl

The first step in airbrushing a waterfowl is to give it a complete undercoat. The undercoating gives a good surface to work on, helps conceal blemishes, and allows other colors to cover more completely. Each bird will have a color that is predominate, and you must decide what it is. For the male teal that we are doing, it is a light gray. The female teal is a chocolate brown, and a Canadian goose will do best with a light gray. To apply the undercoat, open the brush to its maximum setting for good coverage.

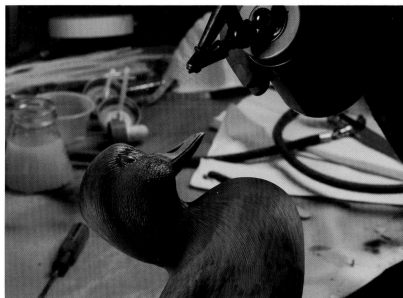

You can start anywhere, but be sure to turn the bird in every angle to insure complete coverage.

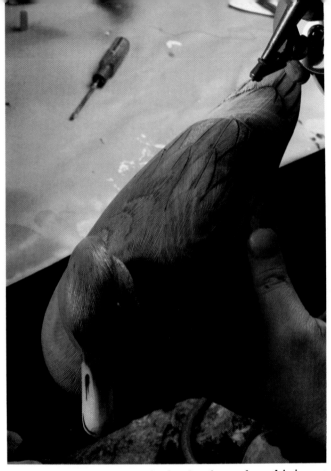

Continue over the whole body. On the male teal it is not necessary to do the bill because it will be painted black and is a smooth enough surface to take the paint well.

After the undercoat we add the color to the bird. On the teal we begin with burnt sienna for the head. I like to begin with the head, because we always get overspray onto the body. I try to approach the head from the back to reduce the amount of overspraying. Depending on the consistency of the paint, I usually open the nozzle about half-way. Remember there is a gray band between the head and the chest so leave enough gray.

The head has a lot of texture, so you need to be sure to use enough paint to cover completely. No gray should show through.

The head with raw sienna. It will have a burnt umber crest, but I will wait to do that when I apply burnt umber to other parts of the bird. This is a time saver, saving one or two color changes.

Check the head from all angles and be sure every thing is covered.

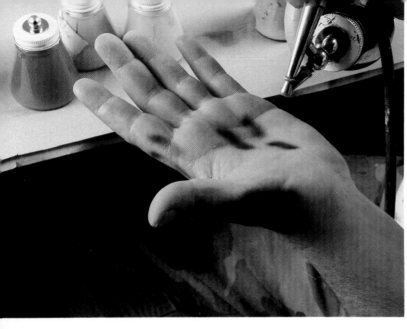

Begin with the coverts. I start in the middle in case there is a blob of paint in the needle.

The next color for the teal is black for the rump. I generally follow the same order for any bird: head, rump, back, sides, and chest. I close the brush down for this to avoid overspraying. My hand makes a good testing block.

Work along the edge of the coverts to the outside. Point the brush a little ways from the edge and use a jiggling motion to bring the paint up to the edge.

Paint along the channel.

Fill in between the channel and the edge of the coverts.

Paint along the ball line...

and the tail line.

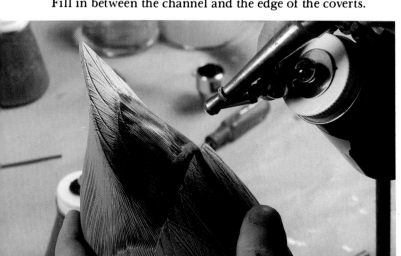

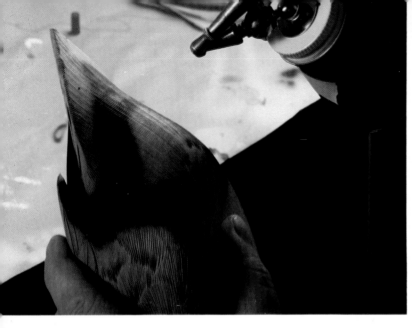

Fill in the under-rump area.

While we are using the black we will do the bill. Dial the brush down even more to avoid overspraying onto the head. With it almost closed, begin with the culmen...

and work down the sides...

and underneath.

Progress so far.

When the edge along the head is done, open the brush and fill in to the tip.

When painting the head we got some overspray.

Return to gray to cover.

With burnt umber and the tip closed down, begin at the front of the crown and ...

work your way back along the edge...

to the back of the head. This defines the blend lines

When I apply paint to the crown, I move the brush in a sweeping motion that follows the lines of the feathers, giving it a truer line.

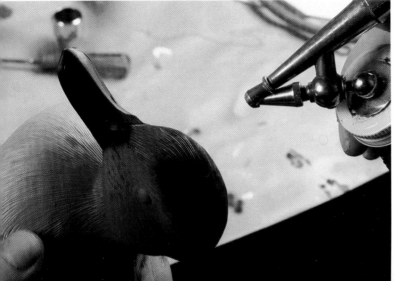

Open the tip and fill in the crown area.

Even though you are misting, you want to achieve an even coverage.

Open the tip more and holding the brush 6-8 inches away, mist the shoulder area back to the tertials.

When you dial your tip from a large opening to a small opening, your first blast is going to be a splatter—every time. Use a piece of paper towel or scrap to absorb this problem.

To paint the tertials, dial the brush down, and, holding it close to the surface, spray along the quill.

Continue with burnt umber on the tail. Open your gun and start on the edges.

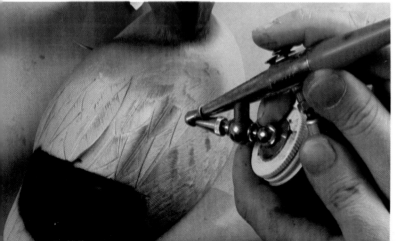

Gradually back the brush away and continue to spray the tertials, giving it a blended appearance.

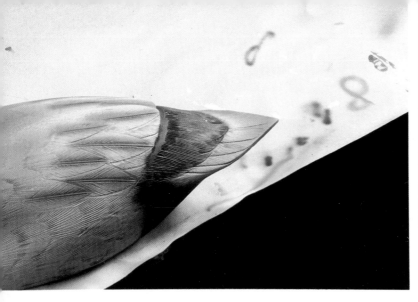

When you don't clean all the color out of your brush, you end up with a mixture that could spoil your work. The yellow band at the bottom is the color we are looking for. The yellow patch under the rump is yellow ocher with a touch of white.

Work your way toward the coverts, but leave some gray between the black and the burnt umber.

Make two big blots of yellow by outlining...

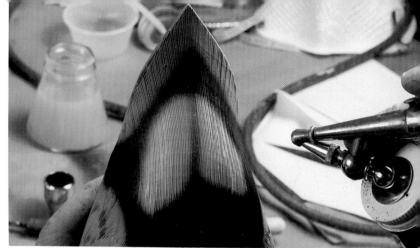

then filling.

Place one blot on each side.

Go back to black paint and clean up the edges of the yellow...

so you end up with two nice yellow markings.

Moving to the chest we use a peach mixed from burnt sienna, raw sienna and white. With your tipped closed down, start one-half inch below the raw sienna neck line and create a line to either side over to about one inch from the ball.

Bring a line down and back.

Fade the edges into the gray.

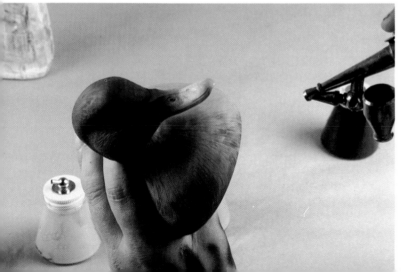

Fill in the chest area, being sure to cover the gray completely.

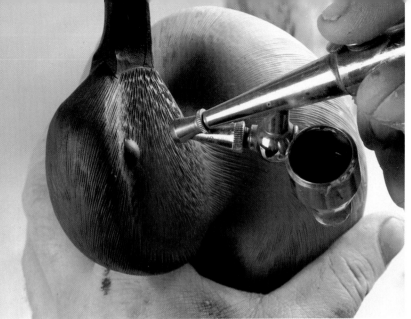

Use thalo green for the eye patch. Because I am only using a small amount, I use a cup instead of a jar. This is one of the hardest colors to clean out of your gun, so clean it immediately after using. To avoid overspray, close the tip all the way, and then open it until only a small amount of paint comes out. Start at the center...

and work your way back. With the tip closed this much, you are going to have to keep opening it slightly as you work. This is because the paint dries and makes the opening even smaller as you go.

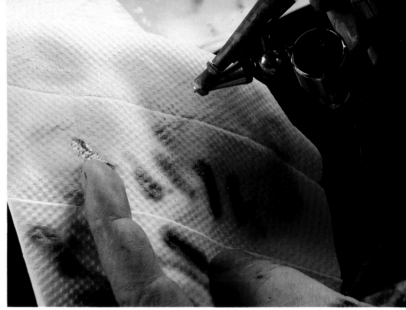

Over the thalo green we add irridescent green. With all iridescent paints close the tip as much as possible, because they splatter easily. I use a piece of towel to test my adjustments.

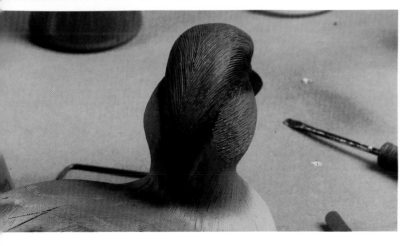

The results.

Start at the eye...

With burnt umber we will add spots to the chest, using the technique discussed earlier. Again, use a towel to adjust the tip.

and work you way back covering the thalo green completely. The combination of the two greens gives the color depth and realism.

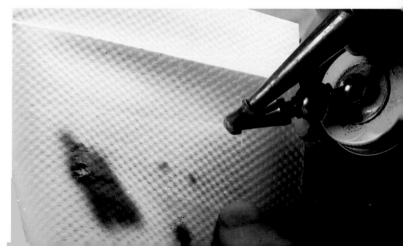

It is also helpful to practice a little on a piece of cardboard or scrap to get the size you want.

Continue across the breast.

Avoid creating a pattern to the dots. Also vary the size of the dots and the intensity of the color.

The interiors highlighted with white.

Next we move to the white interiors of the side feathers. White is the color that will give you the most trouble. No matter what you do it will splatter and overspray. In the case of feather interiors it doesn't matter much because we will paint over it later. But if you are doing a large area, you should use the white first. With the gun almost closed and holding it about an inch and one half away from the surface, highlight the interior of each side feather.

Use raw sienna to lighten the cheek area from the bill to the eye. Close your brush almost all the way and hold it about an inch from the surface. The color should be more intense toward the bill and fade as it moves back toward the eye.

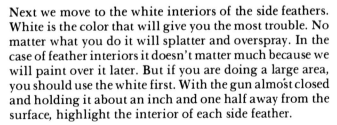

36

It's these subtle colors that give the bird its realism.

For the first edging, place your brush at the edge of the feather...

For some of the details it is necessary to use a brush technique. We use a Grumbacher round red sable series 190 number 8 brush to paint the tertial covert and tertial edgings. The buff color is made by mixing raw sienna and white from the tube. Add enough water to make it workable.

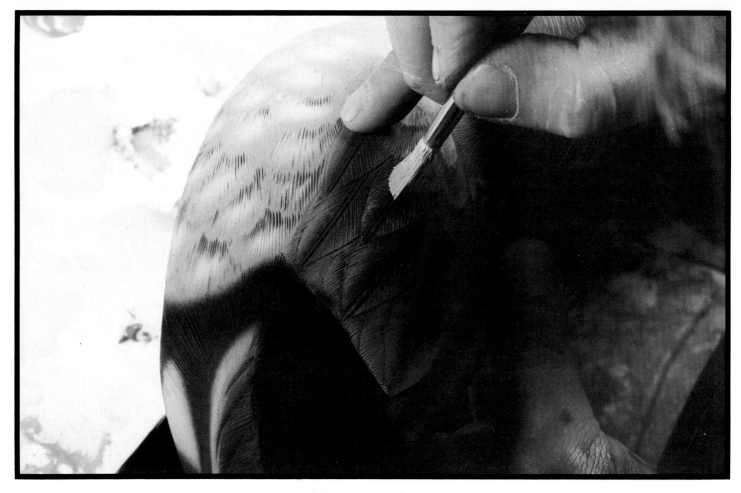

and draw in toward the center.

Over the first edging, make a second edging of white with
a touch of raw sienna.

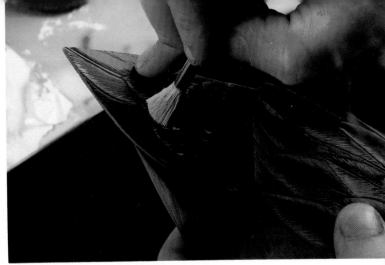

Highlight the edge of the tail coverts...

Make cup feathers on the upper-rump area by flattening your brush in the paint so the bristles fan out, and then placing your brush at the edge of the feather and pulling inward.

and the tail feathers.

Cleaning the Airbrush Tip

Unscrew the color cap from the needle.

Remove the needle.

We finished the whole bird without dismantling the tip, but now it is necessary. Begin by using the Allen wrench provided with the airbrush to loosen the set screw.

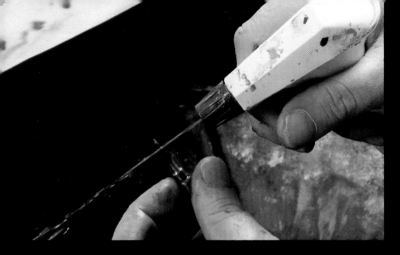

Saturate the needle with 409™.

Clean the tip and the color cap with the pipecleaner.

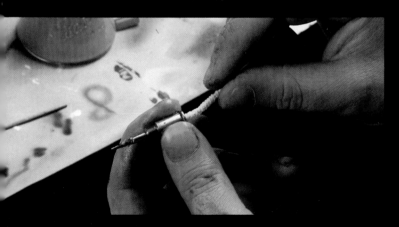

Ream the needle with a pipecleaner.

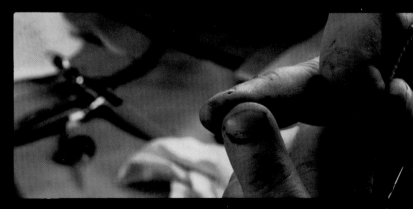

This little speck in the tip was enough to cause us problems.

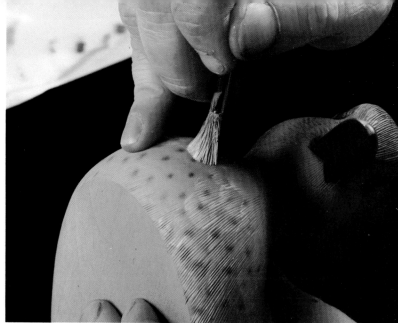

Use the Grumbacher 190 (cup brush) with white paint to create the breast feathers.

Use a mixture of yellow ocher and raw sienna for the eyeline. Using a Robert Simmons series 750 number four script brush, begin at the front of the eye outline the green beneath the eye and bring back the top line from the bill.

The other way to vermiculate uses a Grumbacher 190 (cup brush). We lightly tap the bird to form a series of arcs moving down and to one side. This method also gives a nice result, but is far less time consuming. Count on about one-half hour per bird.

Opposite page:
Vermiculation is an important process for the realism of the bird. One method creates a beautiful pattern, but is quite time consuming. Plan on about four hours per bird. Use a number 4 script brush and a dark paint. On the teal the vermiculation will be done with black paint, while a mallard would be done in brown. Make wavy lines on the sides, the cape area, and the gray band we left on the front.

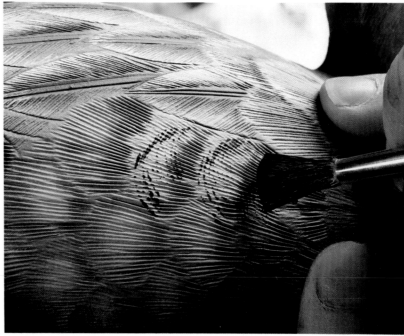

Move your brush forward and to the side to give the layered effect of the feathers.

These patterns accumulate to give this nice effect.

Paint the secondaries using a script brush and iridescent green paint. The brush is easier here because of the danger of overpainting when using a airbrush.

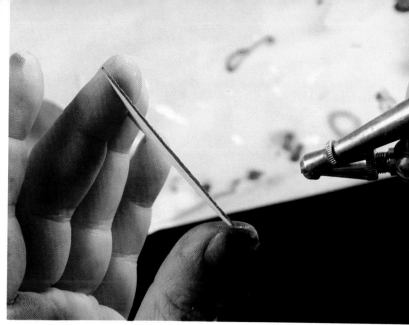

Be sure to cover the edges as well as the back side.

Undercoat the primaries with burnt umber using number 5 tip opened most of the way.

Use light brown (burnt umber and white mixed) and lighten the interior of the primaries.

Lightly dust the trailing edge of primaries with black to help set them off.

Use the script brush to paint the edges of the secondaries.

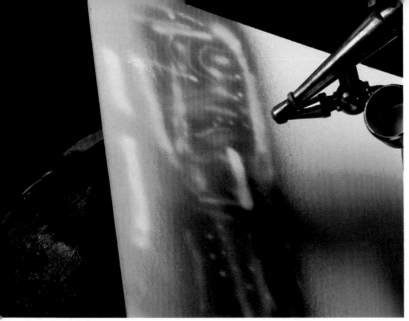

Spray the crescents with straight white. Use a scrap piece to test for width, closing or opening the head as needed.

The crescent should be about ¼'' wide.

50

Clearing a Clog in the Paint Jar

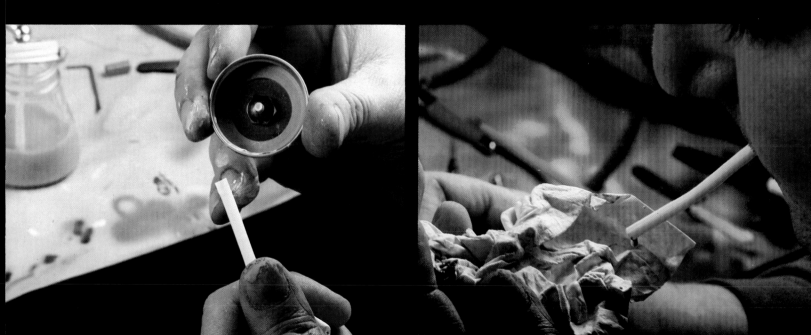

Loosen the nut on the inside of the lid.

Use a pipe cleaner to remove the clog in the knuckle.

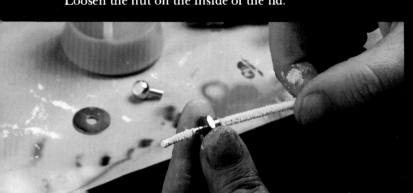

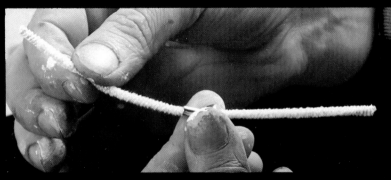

Undercoat the hen with burnt umber, holding the airbrush
6-8 inches away to get wide coverage.

Do the rump to the ball, overspraying so you can create a blend line.

Using a buff color cover the under-rump and the head. Spray the head up to the crown, twisting and turning to assure even coverage. Don't worry about overspraying because we will come back to it with the burnt umber and create a blend line.

Spray out to the edge of the tail.

Try to get a smooth, complete coverage.

Return to the burnt umber for blending. Begin on the crown and cover the buff overpainting.

Bring the blend line just over the edge of the crown using short spurts instead of one long continuous spray.

Blend the bottom of the neck and the breast.

Starting at the bill create the eye line.

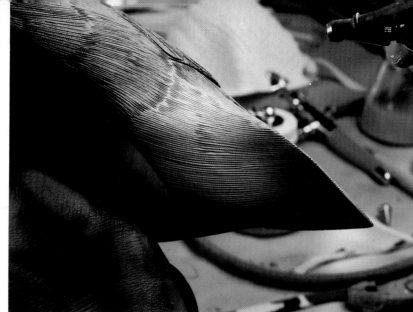

Paint your blend line....

Clean up over sprays in the rump area.

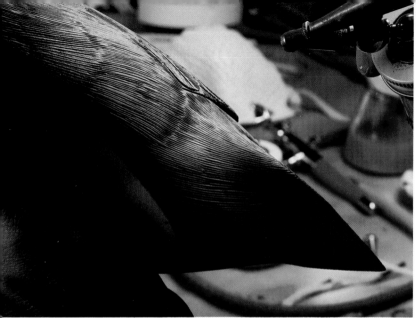

I have some buff overspray on the edge of the tail.

and fill in behind it. Be careful not to create a line.

To cover this I spray down on the tail with burnt umber.

This paints the edge without overpainting the bottom. Before putting the burnt umber away, paint the primaries.

then back away to get wider coverage.

Use the same light brown that was used on the interiors of the drake primaries to highlight the interiors of the hen tertials and tertial coverts. On the tertials come in close to do the quill...

Hold the airbrush about 4 inches from the edge of the tail and mist it with light brown.

On the coverts lightly spray the centers.

Use the script brush and burnt umber to streak the buff area of the head...

and rump. The pattern is not as tight on the rump and there are some spots.

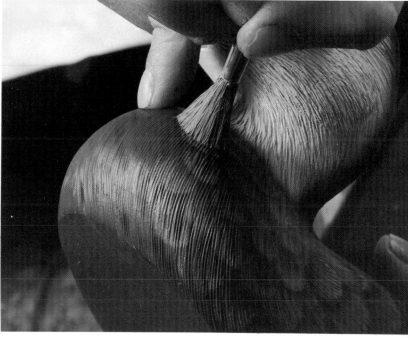

Edge the chest and side feathers in raw sienna mixed with a little white.

continue with the tertial coverts...

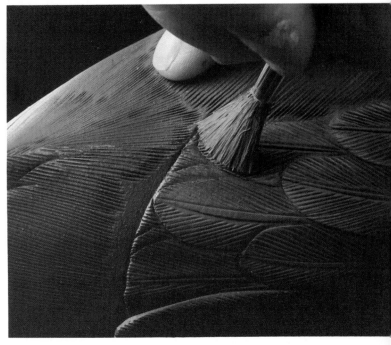

tertials...

and tail feathers.

Now you are almost finished with the painting. It is important now to be sure your hands are clean or you may pay a dear price. Cut around the eye with a knife...

Do a second edging in all four areas using white paint mixed with a little raw sienna.

Apply gloss medium and varnish to the bill.

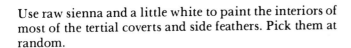

and peel the paint off.

Use raw sienna and a little white to paint the interiors of most of the tertial coverts and side feathers. Pick them at random.

Paint the secondaries iridescent green.

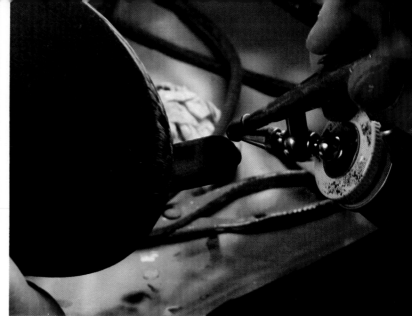

With the airbrush almost closed, apply black to the underside of the bill.

Apply a medium gray undercoat to the hen's bill.

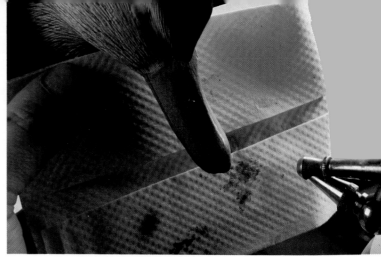

At the end, flare out the painting...

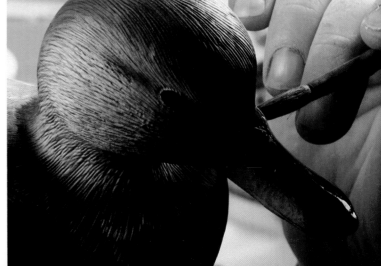

Paint the top of the bill black. Use a towel to protect the chest from the black paint and paint down the center of the bill.

to get this effect.

Use the script brush to apply some black "freckles" to the side of the bill.

A simple wedge holds the primaries in place while the glue dries.

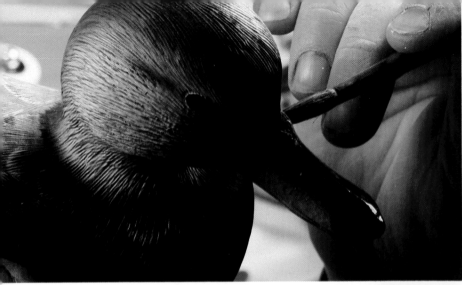

Gloss the bill of the hen....

and we're finished

A Gallery of Details

The drake.

Bill detail.

The head detail.

Shoulder detail.

Tail detail.

Side view.

Chest detail.

The under-rump.

The hen.

The head.

The bill.

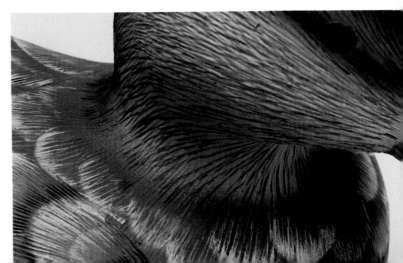

The neck and shoulder.

The shoulder.

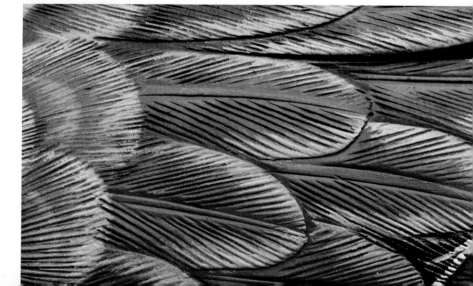

The back.

Primaries.

The tail.

The end.

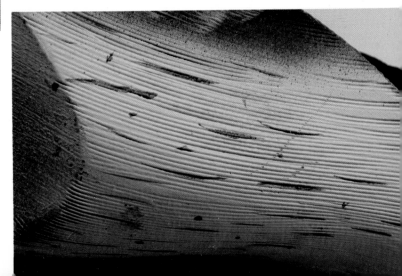